Dedication

 For my Elders of the Kitfield Village

 For my siblings (Abraham and Sarah's Children)

 For my darling Hack

 For my children, grandchildren, and great grandchildren

 For my dear friends and friends who have encouraged the birthing of this book,

I love you all dearly and dedicate this book to you all for you have inspired the makings of this book in some way or another.

A special thank you to Willis Sanders for the beautiful artwork used on the cover of the book and Sasha Wright with Writers Block SC for helping me bring this dream into fruition.

Jewels From the Heart

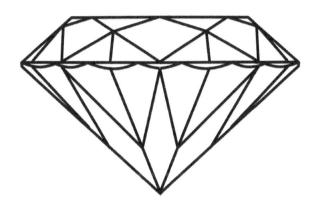

By Julia Wright

Jul's Jewels

For me, accepting differences is the spice of life! Listening and learning from someone who doesn't think like I do, expands my knowledge. I shall forever remain open to another, discounting no one! I enjoy watching the buzzards circling in the air just as much as I enjoy the wild doves pecking on the ground around the bird feeders. I have experienced much kindness and help from the addict, and the drunk. Everyone and everything teaches! Forever learning!

Take a moment to reflect and write about a time when you learned something from someone who thought differently than you? What were your "takeaways"? How did it change your life?

Jul's Jewels

- It's okay to be unpredictable! Yes, I rode in a Hot Air Balloon over the West Bank of Luxor in Egypt!

- Seeing beautiful flowers in a stranger's yard some years back, helped me at a time that I was growing through a scary time in my life! So, I share with joy, this space!

- Grateful to be an integral part of the fabric of LIFE.. even more grateful to know it's nothing to earn; but a Gift, allowing LIFE to express ITSELF through me, in me, as me!

Take a moment to reflect and write about a time when you were able to share joy in nature?

Jul's Jewels

I am learning, I am just where I need to be at that moment, even if the place feels uncomfortable! What I know at that point then becomes, what is it that I must learn? Earth School is real, not abstract! ISP! There is an Individual Spiritual Plan for us all, not planned by man!

May we continue to die to old patterns and thoughts and allow the resurrected Spirit of LOVE to flow through us! "And I saw a new Heaven and a new Earth for the old had passed away".

Take a moment to reflect and write about a time when you questioned if you were where you were meant to be in life? What was your aha moment to know you were where you were meant to be?

Jul's Jewels

It feels great when one gets to that place where one doesn't have to justify or defend one's NO or YES!

While sitting and having breakfast, I realized that I don't want to take anything for granted, not even the fork and plate! Too much to enumerate! I am so grateful for Divine Symbiosis!

Take a moment to reflect and write about a time when you felt freedom from just saying no or yes without any justification.

Jul's Jewels

Only twenty-six letters in the alphabets, and the power of each letter is remarkable! Can you imagine the power of humanity as we connect practicing the golden rule? There is an African Proverb that says, "when spider-webs connect even spider-webs can tie up elephants". Keep allowing and less striving!!!

Take a moment to reflect and write about a time you connected with someone or others to accomplish a task and it went well?

Jul's Jewels

♦ Love loves company, so does misery! Are you great company with yourself?

♦ Just had an epiphany while cleaning!! Do you think cleaning is a calling? I am glad it called me today!

♦ In God, all things are possible, In spite of appearances. Believing must transcend to a knowing. Walk in wellness.....mind, body, and soul!

Take a moment to reflect and write about how you view yourself? Are you pleasant company?

Jul's Jewels

Listening to the roll call of birds is such a joy! It's like the leader starts, and then from a distance you hear another, and then another! They aren't trying to outdo another. They rejoice because they hear themselves in each other! Oh, how all of Creations speak! I rejoice in saying, good morning, good day, good evening, good night! Let it all be good to you and for you this day!

Take a moment to reflect and write about a time you found your voice in someone else?

Jul's Jewels

 I buried yesterday and arose this morning with an openness to receive with gratitude today's offerings. Grateful for daily resurrections as I die to the past! Keep allowing and less striving!!!

 You are abundant life, for within you flow the Essence of LIFE!! Keep allowing and less striving!!

I just told my left hand, "put that down, you don't need to put another thing in my mouth to eat tonight"! And it listened!

Take a moment to reflect and write about what you are grateful for today.

Jul's Jewels

◆ **Fear LESS, love MORE, and become attentive to what happens to you, through you, in you, as you, throughout the day. May you experience a joy-FULL, peace-FULL day! Keep allowing and less striving!!**

◆ **To Light up the Universe begins with each of us! UniVerse! Your voice does matter! The DIRECTOR wants harmony!**

 It's okay to have a sense of humor without feeling guilty in spite of the seriousness of what the world is currently facing!

Take a moment to reflect and write about something you will do to let your light shine and your voice be heard.

Jul's Jewels

For me, I am learning, it is not only in the reading, but in the living. Life is experiencing the moment! To only describe "banana" gives me no substance. LIFE is an experiential walk. Allowing LIFE to experience ITSELF in you, through you, as you is an humbling experience! Oh so Grateful for the gift of LIFE!

It's never too late to do a good deed too soon!

Take a moment to reflect and write about a time you let your hair down and just experienced the moment before you.

Jul's Jewels

These are the best of times and the worst of times; the times that will try the soul! We are more than meet the eyes (I's)! So grateful that the whole world is being turned by God, and that this is not a soap opera! God bless the Universe!

Homemade chicken soup is good for the body, thus, allows the soul to smile!

Take a moment to reflect and write about a time that tried your soul.

Jul's Jewels

I honor My Mother, Annie Bertha, Sis, Freddie Momma, Gramma Sukie, Annie Daisy, Cun Ida, Cun Beauty, Annie Hattie, Cun Rachael, Cun Sarah Bartley, Cun, Mozell, Annie Babe, Cun Miss, Cun Milla, Cun Nancy, Eurlean, Mabel, and ALL of the women of the KITFIELD VILLAGE! These women were prayer warriors, quilters, natural comedians, waymakers, mistakes makers, sharers, gardeners, brilliant, these hidden figures were every woman! YES, everywoman! They might not have had much schooling, BUT, oh they were educated! Educated by the Essence of Life! These women didn't profess to be professors! However, as a Kitfieldian, I confer posthumously upon these women the greatest degree in my opinion, the degree of TEACHING MOTHERS! Awomen!

Take a moment to reflect and write about the teaching mothers in your life. Who are they and what are you grateful for about them?

Jul's Jewels

♦ Grateful for the ubiquitous element water that cleanses and quenches! Do you think the green grass that's watered by the dew first thing in the
morning is reminding us to also water our bodies once we are awaken?
#Justathought#gratefulforwater!

♦ Pay know mind to the mind...unless it's renewed!

Take a moment to reflect and write about the many benefits of water in your life.

Jul's Jewels

I am so grateful that I went to see the mesmerizing, electrifying movie, HIDDEN FIGURES and learned of Katherine Johnson! What a mathematical genius! John Glenn wasn't going to orbit the planet without Mrs. Johnson verifying the calculations of a nascent NASA computer, an IBM 7090. This verification was done manually! "Our office computed all the (rocket) trajectories," Johnson told the Virginian-pilot newspaper in 2012. "You tell me when and where you want it to come down, and I will tell you where and when and how to launch it." She died during Black History Month at the age of 101 and a few days after the anniversary of John Glenn's orbits of the earth on Feb. 20, 1962! What a gift to the Universe and a testament that nothing hidden that won't be revealed! I salute all of the Hidden Figures! Mrs. Katherine Johnson, you will be remembered by so many, especially the NASA Family!

Take a moment to reflect and write about a black historical figure that made an impact on your life.

Jul's Jewels

 The expression "Every shut eye ain't sleep and every goodbye ain't gone" was birthed out of a strong desire to survive by our ancestors. Oh, how I honor their wisdom, perseverance, and strength! We marinate in the hearts and stand on the shoulders of geniuses. We are their extensions, ya'll!!! Have a mindful day!

 Change is inevitable but misery is optional!

Take a moment to reflect and write about what wisdom you honor from your ancestors or elders.

Jul's Jewels

- **I AM WE!**
  African Proverb...So powerful!

- I am looking forward to the unfolding of a beautiful today. As I look for the good, I begin by saying, good morning, good people!

- Acknowledging another human being is one of the greatest gifts one can give to another human being.....a nod, a smile, or good morning, good evening! Like it or not, we are all related! It's called **HUEMANITY!**

Take a moment to reflect and write about the good you noticed today or in the past week.

Jul's Jewels

- ◆ **There is nothing new under the sun, just some new ways of saying some old things!**

- ◆ **Stop! Look! Listen! Feel the beat of your heart! Annnnnd give yourself a hug!**

- ◆ **Paying attention to the seasons can teach us so much! Change is a natural process. Trusting the process is necessary for growth!**

- ◆ **My to do list:**
  BE!

Take a moment to reflect and write about a time you had to trust the process of change for growth.

Jul's Jewels

In celebrating Black History Month, I salute my parents, the late Abraham & Sarah, along with the Kitfield Village! They taught us how to laugh, play, and pray. Oh, I can't forget and how to share! When one had all had....from a cup of rice to a cup of sugar. Our village was not a cliche! They all reared us. They all could spank us but they all also loved us. And another thing, I celebrate Black History every day....Her-story!
The world is a village!

Take a moment to reflect and write about your ideal village.
What would it look like? How could you contribute to a village?

Jul's Jewels

Can anything good come out of Cross! You bet! Check out the Coach, Rod Wilson for the Kansas City Chiefs! Home grown..home fed! Straight outta Cross High School! They keep coming and standing out in all careers. Yep! An extension of Zion School and Central High! We will continue to rise because no one can keep a great rural town down.... where all the women are strong...all the men are good looking..and where all the children are making a difference!

On my way to exercise this morning, I witnessed a young man at his bus stop doing push ups while waiting for his bus. I smiled and said to myself, that's good news, report it! Here is an eyewitness account! Reporting live from W-CROSS-SC--SHORTCUT RD.

Take a moment to reflect and write about a time you continued to rise despite what was going on around you.

Jul's Jewels

Every day is different, isn't it! That's why the day doesn't make you, you help make it! The difference is, you can't do anything about the hours, but you can make a difference in what happens in the hours! Grateful for this minute in this hour!

WOW!! ♥I just love how LIFE supports us! There are no cheat sheets on this journey!

Take a moment to reflect and write about what you can do to make a difference in your day today or tomorrow.

Jul's Jewels

◆ **NEVER** underestimate a grain of Truth, the return is immeasurable! Oh, what a terrible WEB we weave when we tend to deceive! The world is *UN-WEBBING...TRUTH is marching on! Despite the appearance, I choose to trust the Divine Process! *Julia's Lexicon

 Grateful that I don't have to remind myself to breathe! The BREATH of LIFE does it through me, in me, as me! Grateful to be a conduit, and for the gift of recognition!

Take a moment to reflect and write about a time you were deceived or you deceived someone. How did you feel before, during, and after?

Jul's Jewels

Being a part of the 10,000 things, had to have started with the 1 thing; therefore, the 50th thing, can't say to the 1 thing, "you aren't important as I am because I am larger.....and the 10,000th thing can't say to the 200th thing, I am better because I am the largest."

It took each number to get to the 10,000 things. Each needed each other. So, there are no superlatives on this journey.....good, better, best or holy, holier, holiest. Aren't you glad to be in the number 1 more time!!!!!

Take a moment to reflect and write about a time you realized you weren't better than someone else in a situation.

Jul's Jewels

◆ When Dis-Ease shows up, be gentle with it. It wants to be attended to, for it doesn't want to become a Disease! Being gentle and kind to oneself doeth good like a medicine!

◆ Nothing in the World is more Dangerous than Sincere Ignorance and Conscientious Stupidity"
Dr. Martin Luther King

◆ When we change the lens of our eyes (I's) to WE, we will quickly learn that no one, ABSOLUTELY no one loses on this Spiritual journey, for it is IMPOSSIBLE for LOVE to fail ITSELF!!!!!

Take a moment to reflect and write about a time when you experienced sincere ignorance or conscientious stupidity. How did you handle it?

Jul's Jewels

- ♦ LIFE is like winning the lottery without purchasing a ticket! Grateful!

- ♦ Just love the magic of Earth's abundance! Grateful!!

- ♦ Often times one doesn't recognize a real Revival when it comes. One tends to look for it in a building! A world revival is happening! Jesus often said to his disciples, "Those who have eyes to see, let them see". Many look but few see! Grateful for The greatest TEACHER/GURU...LIFE!

Take a moment to reflect and write about a time when you experienced good fortune in life that you did not do any work for.

Jul's Jewels

I walk in the acceptance of who I am daily...for I am who I am because of I AM! We either speak life or death upon ourselves. I am abundant Life!

I will no longer miss the process of this beautiful Divine living in this present moment, trying to understand it better in the by and by. The by and by is an illusion! Raise your hand in the classroom of LIFE this day and say, "PRESENT"! The INNER ME creates no enemy! Have a FUNTASTIC day!

Take a moment to reflect and write about a time you realized you were missing the process in a moment. How did you feel when you came alive and present in the moment?

Jul's Jewels

A New Year! A New Thinking! A New Result! If we continue to say the same OLD thing, then we will always get the same Old thing. Just maybe, just maybe, the Old Brainwash, may need a New Washing! You and only you have the Power Within to allow the washing to be done!!!! Have a magical, and an enjoyable New Year....one day at a time!!!

Take a moment to reflect and write about a time you started fresh in your thinking.

Jul's Jewels

 "Every tub must sit on its own bottom." ♥ My mother might not have been schooled BUT was educated by the essence of LIFE. Her words are buried deep in my soul! ♥ Oh, do they make so much sense the older I get!!

 When you find yourself in a state of an EMERGENCY, HEAR the alarm....you are EMERGING to another state of GREATNESS, whether it feels like it or not!!!! May you continue to recognize and walk in the blessings of I AM daily!

Take a moment to reflect and write about sayings you heard growing up that make more sense the older you get.

Jul's Jewels

◆ The two most powerful motivations are Love and fear, But remember the Breath that was breathed into you came from Love! So, where does fear come from? Remember, even fear doesn't want to be scared. Love it to life! The Spirit of God within is that of Love, power, and a sound mind! So be motivated by Love!!

◆ Waiting for someone to make your day is like waiting for someone to breathe for you. .Impossible! In Joy, enjoy your day!

Take a moment to reflect and write about a time you were motivated by fear or love. Which one allowed you to be more productive?

Jul's Jewels

ABUN(DANCE)!

I dance with LIFE in ITS fullness! Where IT leads me I gladly follow for it is always for my good and for the good of the whole! In JOY, I dance!

More than, less than, greater than, and equal to are mathematical symbols..on LIFE's journey there is no better than. When you meet the REAL YOU, then YOU will respect everything and everyone around you.

Take a moment to reflect and write about a time you just danced and enjoyed it.

Jul's Jewels

- ◇ **Smile! You are on Universe camera! Yep! Just saw your smile!**

- ◇ **WORTHINESS is a Gift, a gift you can't buy or earn. So grateful!!**

- ◇ **If All of us knew to do better All of the time, then All of us would do better All of the time. Oh how grateful I am for GRACE!**

- ◇ **Often times, I am amazed that I am amaze....yet, I desire to continue to be amazed of how amazing LIFE is....**

Take a moment to reflect and write about the last time you found yourself smiling to yourself.

Jul's Jewels

I have entered the school of UNLEARNING! As I unlearn, I have learned that jealousy, envy, judging, gossiping, racism, competing, etc. are learned behaviors. Oh, am I thrilled to be in the school of UNLEARNING, where the Teacher wield loves unconditionally with no pass or failing grades....just words of encouragement!

Take a moment to reflect and write about a time you had to unlearn something. What was that process like?

Jul's Jewels

◆ When you find yourself trying so hard, take a deep breath and JUST BE!

◆ I love that every day is a fresh start, actually, every moment is a fresh start! Be kind to you moment by moment!

◆ SACRED or Scared.....*C* the difference! From what place do you navigate?

◆ My daddy would give, using his vernacular, "justdrylongso". What a random act of kindness! Let's give sometimes, justdrylongso!

Take a moment to reflect and write about a time you were trying hard to accomplish something and you realized you needed to just let it be.

Jul's Jewels

Darkness is a matter of perspective don't you think....after all, to see the beauty of the stars requires darkness, the seeds for planting welcome the dark soil for growth, and what about a good night's sleep ...I certainly prefer a dark room. The taste of a piece of chocolate is oh so delicious! And awww, what about my dark beautiful hue! I am grateful to be you-niquely designed by the great Divine! So grateful to see this day, and on that note, I am going to get up and enjoy a cup of dark chocolate! In JOY, enjoy your day!

Take a moment to reflect and write about a time you thought you were in darkness but you were actually in a position to grow..

Jul's Jewels

- ◆ It's not what's on my mind BUT what's in my heart.

- ◆ Granted, don't take yourself for granted! There is a Divine Yeast within that continues to Rise!?

- ◆ In the game of LIFE, there is no competition! You are the trophy if you need one!

- ◆ There is no losing on this journey of LIFE, just as the GPS system recalibrates and takes you where you so desire, so does LIFE!

Take a moment to reflect and write about what's on your heart today.

Jul's Jewels

I AM thankful for Laughter! It just feels so Good! I had an "I Love Lucy" experience trying to ring my brother's doorbell only to learn they were gadgets to opening his garage doors! One would go up and the other would go down and then, they both went up! I tried closing them both and obviously they were tired, so they just stayed up! I stood there and laughed at myself so hard, laughed so hard that water was coming out of my eyes! I finally called him using my cell phone and he said, "girl, just meet me at the front door!" I couldn't hold the other water, so I went straight to the bathroom! What did I do......laughed some more....and what am I doing now....yes...laughing at myself! YES! I AM THANKFUL FOR LAUGHTER!

Take a moment to reflect and write about a silly moment that moved you to belly laughter.

Jul's Jewels

 When we celebrate the success of each other we all succeed! It's enough for all; after all, success is relative!

 Our arms and hands were created to SERVE each other....not to hurt and harm. SO, let us serve KINDNESS today!

 Confident because of the oneness within of whom I abide and confide! Sooo grateful!

Take a moment to reflect and write about a time you celebrated someone else's success or a time when someone celebrated your success.

Jul's Jewels

◆ The world needs "WOMENARIES"..women who are ready to bring healing to themselves and each other. And to help bring healing to Humanity!

◆ Cross High is full of great surprises! Can anything good come out of Cross...You bet! Just look around…

◆ Nothing goes to waste...for even wastes become soil to the Earth!

◆ LOVE keeps no record!

Take a moment to reflect and write about a "womanary" in your life or a time you have been a "womanary" in someone else's life.

Jul's Jewels

♦ Human on purpose..devinely designed. Oh how Great Thou Art! You are a Masterpiece. May you walk in peace this day.

♦ You are the beneficiary of every word you speak! LIFE has no opposite!

♦ Don't knock a thing because you may not understand it....that same thing you knock may end up being your picker upper!

Take a moment to reflect and make a list of at least 5 things you love about yourself.

Jul's Jewels

◆ It's nothing like a contented heart and a full stomach! Life is good! So grateful for the gift of breath!

◆ I believe everyone and everything is a teacher; especially, children and animals!

◆ When you believe IT, then will you see IT! Grateful for the gift of recognition!

Take a moment to reflect and write about a time you basked in a full stomach and love.

Jul's Jewels

A coward and a bully need each other; perhaps, they are one and the same. However, each needs to acknowledge fear and to help each other to transform that fear! Speaking truth to self is transformative. Let's help each other bring the best out of each other!

Where Divine LOVE flows fear goes!

Take a moment to reflect and speak truth into your own self.

# Jul's Jewels

♦ **Blessings often times come in disguise, be mindful not to discount anyone, especially those who may not talk or look like you!**

♦ **Counting one to a hundred means you must begin with one. Ninety-nine can't say that it's more important than one! You count! No one is bigger than you on this journey of LIFE!**

♦ **LESS is MORE! It was through less that I found MORE! Have an insightful day!**

Take a moment to reflect and write about a blessing in disguise that you have experienced.

Jul's Jewels

- ♦ The Divine Universe looks out for all of us all of the time! No exception! The challenge often time is recognizing it!

- ♦ So grateful that I am learning not to rehearse yesterday, and cannot practice tomorrow! #Unlearning!

- ♦ So grateful for LIFE and ITS offerings! To enunciate is like trying to count grains of sands!

Take a moment to reflect and write about a time you felt the universe was looking out for you.

Jul's Jewels

- ♦ The plague from Egypt has landed in our backyard! There are one million Love Bugs flying around. I am an honest liar!

- ♦ As long as there is a NEED for another to ALWAYS feed you on this journey, you could possibly always remain hungry!

- ♦ LIFE needs no additives like can and frozen vegetables! It is just pure! Loving LIFE with a passion!

- ♦ Being kind to yourself strengthens your heart muscle!!!!!

Take a moment to reflect and write about a time you heard the most ridiculous lie.

Jul's Jewels

- LIFE is a LOVE walk, not a convoluted kind of love, but a love where in NO is NO and YES is YES! Have a LOVE walk day!

- A weapon of mass destruction....the tongue....A weapon of mass construction....the tongue. Wow!! Consider this powerful weapon!!!!

- What I know for sure; for me, it is not in the reading, or writing, or the posting, but the satisfaction is in the listening, receiving, and sharing! Be an intentional listener without judging self or another.

Take a moment to reflect and write about how you can walk in love today or tomorrow. What does walking in love look like for you?

Jul's Jewels

◆ **Peace is stillness. As I observe the stillness and the calmness of the trees in our backyard; I am being reminded to respect the sacredness of the environment! Life is symbiotic! Oh how we need each other! May you enjoy the greatness right around your backyard this day!**

◆ **Sometimes we get in our own way on this journey by laboring too hard! REST in the assurance that the Divine never misses a beat!**

Take a moment to and sit in stillness. Observe what you see, hear, feel, and smell. Write down what thoughts come to mind.

Jul's Jewels

The operative number is 49! Yes, it's been forty-nine years this date, August 29th on a Friday, on my mother's birthday, Harry (Hack) and I got married. If you add his forty-nine and my forty-nine, I believe that's 98! Cooray--has it been that long! LOL. To be married to Harry the man, is a fantasy, but to be married to Harry, the soul is a reality. Our relationship keeps evolving. After 49 years, yes, we are still working at not taking each other for granted!. He is bringing the best out of me, and I believe, I am doing the same with him. Grateful for what I am learning and how I am learning!!! To each other be true!!! Love for me is never giving up on each other. Love waits, and waits, and waits some more! 49 years! WOW! With the same man! Forever learning and loving! My HACK!❤

Take a moment to reflect and write about a relationship you've seen or experienced where the love keeps evolving.

Jul's Jewels

♦ Just be, warts and all! Kissing your own warts may just turn you into the princess and prince you were always meant to be!!! Walk in compassion of your weaknesses. Every time you judge you with "I shoulda, coulda, woulda, you punish you! Contrary to learned behaviors, you do deserve the best!

♦ Not in competition with a soul but in cooperation with LIFE! Loving IT!

Take a moment to reflect and make a list of things you think are your weaknesses.

Jul's Jewels

- ♦ **LIFE is for giving! The Joy of it is, IT never runs out, and we are the beneficiaries in the land of the living, daily! Grateful!**

- ♦ **Peace is never measured with another man's yardstick!!! Peace can always be yours in spite of what's happening around you when you remain focused on the Peacegiver within!!! It's okay to make peace with yourself!!!**

Take a moment to reflect and make a list of things in your life that never run out.

Jul's Jewels

♦ **LISTENING! One of the greatest gifts one can give oneself and to another! Study to be quiet!**

♦ **Let IT flow..Let IT flow..Let IT flow! Let IT naturally flow! Nothing forced grown is steady! May your day flow with LOVE! TRUST the Divine Process!**

Take a moment to just listen. Write down what comes to your mind.

Jul's Jewels

- ♦ Walking slowly with another is an empathetic Walk, knowing we are on the same journey but the shoe sizes are just different!

- ♦ Today is Spread Kindness Day! By the way, I just made that up! But isn't it a good idea? And don't forget by giving it to self!

- ♦ JUST TO BE is so freeing..after all we are called Human Being and not Human Doing! It's in the being that the doing gets done!

- ♦ Labeling oneself limits infinite possibilities and for sure don't allow others to label you!

Take a moment to reflect and write about a time when you were limited by your own beliefs. How did you overcome those limitations?

Jul's Jewels

 One can NEVER kill time..so don't call me to kill time! Call because you thought of me at the time!

 Don't defeat yourself by giving up! I don't remember the group's name but the song was "Keep on Pushing, you can't stop now, move up a little higher some way somehow". You got this!

This too shall pass is not a cliche! Nothing comes to stay! Holding on to a memory, good or bad, can block something even better that you can help create this day! Fear (no)thing! Omnipresent/ Omnipotent/ Omniscient/ God is EVERYTHING!

Take a moment to reflect and write about what you need in this moment to keep going?

Jul's Jewels

◆ What one does and the spirit in what one does, speak so LOUDLY, I can barely hear what one says! Are my words contributing to building peace and unity? A question invoked within to ask self....Our words matter!!!

◆ Take (no)thing personal! No one got anywhere by himself/ herself!

◆ Standing on the shoulders of countless! Incredibly grateful!

◆ Trying to manipulate LIFE is like telling yourself when to blink, when to breathe, and telling your heart when to beat! Just be grateful that you are a gift of LIFE. There is nothing to earn...no brownie points! Wheewh! Incredibly Grateful!

Take a moment to reflect and write about how you will continue to make your words matter.

Jul's Jewels

◇ Beware of the danger of always quoting another, or another will never have the opportunity of quoting you! You are an original! If we are all doing the same dance, put your own twist to it...It's Electric! A New Year; A New You; A New Mind!

◇ It just feels darn right good feeling Good! Have a darn right good feeling day! Wow! That just made me SMILE! You did too! Waiting for someone to make your day is like waiting for someone to breathe for you. Impossible! In Joy, enjoy your day!

Take a moment to reflect and write about a time you lost yourself in someone else.

Jul's Jewels

Kindness and love are not defined by age, gender, or race, nor does pain! Many of us may have heard the expressions, "kill two birds with one stone", or "madly in love". Well, by pruning my mind, the expressions have become, "light two candles with one match", and "sanely in love". As a woman or a man thinks and feels, so is she/he! I am grateful!!!!!

Take a moment to reflect and write about what pruning you may need to do in your mind.

Made in the USA
Middletown, DE
15 August 2022

71195312R00066